Intimacy with the Almighty

Four Spiritual Disciplines for Cultivating Closeness with God

A PERSONAL JOURNEY

From the Bible-teaching ministry of

CHARLES R. SWINDOLL

INSIGHT FOR LIVING

Charles R. Swindoll graduated in 1963 from Dallas Theological Seminary, where he now serves as the school's fourth president, helping to prepare a new generation of men and women for the ministry. Chuck has served in pastorates in three states: Massachusetts, Texas, and California, including almost twenty-three years at the First Evangelical Free Church in Fullerton, California. He is currently senior pastor of Stonebriar Community Church in Frisco, Texas, north of Dallas. His sermon messages have been aired over radio since 1979 as the *Insight for Living* broadcast. A best-selling author, he has written numerous books and booklets on many subjects.

Based on the outlines and transcripts of Charles R. Swindoll's sermons, the study guide text was developed and written by the Educational Ministries Department at Insight for Living.

Editor in Chief:
Cynthia Swindoll

Study Guide Writer:
Gary Matlack

Assistant Editor and Writer:
Wendy Peterson

Copy Editors:
Tom Kimber
Marco Salazar

Cover Designer:
Nina Paris

Text Designer:
Gary Lett

Graphics System Administrator:
Bob Haskins

Publishing System Specialist:
Alex Pasieka

Director, Communications Division:
Deedee Snyder

Marketing Manager:
Alene Cooper

Project Coordinator:
Colette Muse

Production Manager:
John Norton

Unless otherwise identified, all Scripture references are from the New American Standard Bible, © The Lockman Foundation 1960, 1962, 1963, 1968, 1971, 1972, 1973, 1975, 1977. Used by permission. Scripture taken from the Holy Bible, New International Version © 1973, 1978, 1984 International Bible Society, used by permission of Zondervan Bible Publishers. Also cited is *The Message: The New Testament in Contemporary English* (Colorado Springs, Colo.: NavPress, 1993).

ISBN 1-57972-004-8
COVER PHOTOGRAPH: NEO Photo, Inc., Jack Fritze, photographer
Printed in the United States of America

CONTENTS

INTRODUCTION

Nobody around me knows this," confided the pastor, "but I'm operating on fumes. I am lonely, hollow, shallow, and enslaved to a schedule that never lets up." As I embraced him and affirmed his vulnerability and honesty, he began to weep with deep, heaving sobs. We prayed before he slipped back into the crowd.

Later, as I reflected on that dear man's struggle, I began to think about why we all feel frayed and frustrated at times on our spiritual journey. The core issue, I'm convinced, is one of intimacy with God.

We can have involvements, activities, and programs aplenty. But if we lack intimacy with the Almighty, life becomes a blur without purpose or direction.

That's why I presented this series. It contains some of my deepest thoughts about how to draw close—and stay close—to our heavenly Father. It's not really a study guide; it's more like a personal journey. So as you walk through it, think, pray, reflect, and write. And turn life's hardest roads into life's greatest adventure.

Chuck Swindoll

PUTTING TRUTH
INTO ACTION

K nowledge apart from application falls short of God's desire for His children. He wants us to apply what we learn so that we will change and grow. This study guide was prepared with these goals in mind. As you go through the following pages, we hope your desire to discover biblical truth will grow as your understanding of God's Word increases and that you will be encouraged to apply what you've learned.

To assist you in your study, we've included a section called Moving toward Intimacy at the end of each lesson. These exercises will challenge you to study further and to think of specific ways to put your discoveries into action.

There are many ways to use this guide—in personal devotions, group studies, discussions with friends and family, and Sunday school classes. And, of course, it's an ideal study aid when you're listening to its corresponding *Insight for Living* radio series.

To benefit most from this study guide, we would encourage you to consider it a spiritual journal. That's why we've included space in the **Moving toward Intimacy** sections for recording your thoughts and discoveries. We hope you'll return to those sections often for review and encouragement as you continue to grow in your walk with Christ.

Gary Matlack

Gary Matlack
Coauthor of Text
Author of Moving toward Intimacy

Intimacy
with the
Almighty

Four Spiritual Disciplines for
Cultivating Closeness with God

Chapter 1

Enjoying Intimacy
with the Almighty

Selected Scriptures

When I consider your heavens,
    the work of your fingers,
the moon and the stars,
    which you have set in place,
what is man that you are mindful of him,
    the son of man that you care for him?
(Ps. 8:3–4 NIV)

Have you ever wondered where David was when he wrote this psalm? Perhaps he was stretched out on a cool patch of grass at night, arms folded behind his head, gazing into the jewel-laden sky above. Or maybe he was standing on a balcony of his palace, looking out on Jerusalem, reminiscing about the God of the universe who had turned a shepherd boy into the king of a nation.

Wherever he was, he was contemplating life's most wondrous— and often most baffling—truth: An infinite Creator in loving relationship with a finite creation. The eternal invading time. Unapproachable purity reaching out to sinful humanity. God Almighty our most intimate friend.

Staying with Our First Love

Never has there been a more beautiful paradox: We can have a close, loving relationship with Almighty God. Yet, because we live in a fallen world, everything around us seems to work against developing intimacy with Him. Jam-packed schedules, financial

1

pressures, and competing values try to distract us from our first love, the Lord Jesus Himself. Even sincere Christians in successful churches can lose sight of what's really important. The apostle John wrote of such a church in the book of Revelation:

> "To the angel of the church in Ephesus write:
> The One who holds the seven stars in His right hand, the One who walks among the seven golden lampstands, says this: 'I know your deeds and your toil and perseverance, and that you cannot endure evil men, and you put to the test those who call themselves apostles, and they are not, and you found them to be false; and you have perseverance and have endured for My name's sake, and have not grown weary. But I have this against you, that you have left your first love.'" (2:1–4)

John R. W. Stott says of the Ephesians, "Their first flush of ecstasy had passed. Their early devotion to Christ had cooled. They had been in love with Him, but they had fallen out of love."[1]

It can happen today too. Christ can become obscured in the dust of religious busyness, and we can lose sight of Him. He seems distant, uninvolved. But it doesn't have to be, or stay, that way. Whether you're adrift from God or simply looking for ways to stay close to Him and keep from drifting, you'll find encouragement in these lessons.

Intimacy Defined

Intimacy with the Almighty, then, is our goal. But before we pursue it, we had better define it. Being *intimate*, says Webster, means

> belonging to or characterizing one's deepest nature
> . . . marked by very close association, contact, or
> familiarity . . . marked by a warm friendship de-
> veloping through long association.[2]

Think about your closest relationships. The people with whom you can bare your heart and soul without fear of being judged or rejected. Those who know you best . . . and love you anyway.

---

1. John R. W. Stott, *What Christ Thinks of the Church* (Grand Rapids, Mich.: William B. Eerdmans Publishing Co., 1958), p. 27.

2. *Merriam-Webster's Collegiate Dictionary*, 10th ed., see "intimate."

Those relationships took time to develop, didn't they? They require work and dedication to maintain.

Likewise, intimacy with God takes commitment. It won't happen naturally, automatically, quickly, or easily. Quick-fix formulas make for a shallow, superficial faith. As author Richard Foster says, we already have enough of that.

> Superficiality is the curse of our age. The doctrine of instant satisfaction is a primary spiritual problem. The desperate need today is not for a greater number of intelligent people, or gifted people, but for deep people.[3]

The ongoing process of deepening our walk with God comprises many elements, some of which we can't plan or package. For example, God may allow suffering to occur in our lives to deepen us. Or He might bring an unexpected blessing, showing a facet of His character that we needed to see.

But often we have a definite responsibility in cultivating closeness with God. James says, "Draw near to God and He will draw near to you" (James 4:8a). And our part in drawing near involves discipline.

Discipline: An Important Part of the Process

Don't let the word *discipline* scare you. The Greek concept simply means "to train." It pictures an athlete in preparation for the games. Paul said to Timothy,

> Discipline yourself for the purpose of godliness; for bodily discipline is only of little profit, but godliness is profitable for all things, since it holds promise for the present life and also for the life to come. (1 Tim. 4:7b–8)

Or as Eugene Peterson rendered it, "Exercise daily in God—no spiritual flabbiness, please! Workouts in the gymnasium are useful, but a disciplined life in God is far more so, making you fit both today and forever."[4]

Discipline, in other words, says to us, "Make it a priority, stick with it, don't approach it casually."

3. Richard J. Foster, *Celebration of Discipline: The Path to Spiritual Growth* (San Francisco, Calif.: Harper and Row, Publishers, 1978), p. 1.

4. Eugene H. Peterson, *The Message: The New Testament in Contemporary English* (Colorado Springs, Colo.: NavPress, 1993), p. 442.

3

In the next three lessons, we'll focus on four spiritual disciplines for cultivating intimacy with our Lord:

- simplicity, which requires reordering our lives

- silence, which asks us to be still

- solitude, which involves cultivating serenity

- surrender, which beckons us to let go

So get ready. You may discover that you need to make a few changes in your life. For God will not always speed up to catch up with us. He expects us to slow our pace to walk with Him. God will not always scream and shout because life is noisy. He expects us to provide some quietness where His still and small voice can be heard. God will not be squeezed into the framework of our complicated schedules. We must adjust and adapt to His style and meet His expectations for there to be intimacy—where hearts are shared and closeness results in true godliness.

God Wants Intimacy with Us

With all this talk about discipline, we might have you thinking that developing intimacy with God is completely up to us. It's not. As much as we may want intimacy with God, He wants intimacy with us even more. In fact, as J. I. Packer explains, He took the initiative in establishing intimacy with us.

> What matters supremely, therefore, is not, in the last analysis, the fact that I know God, but the larger fact which underlies it—that fact that he knows me. I am graven on the palms of his hands. I am never out of his mind. All my knowledge of him depends on his sustained initiative in knowing me. I know him because he first knew me, and continues to know me. He knows me as a friend, one who loves me; and there is no moment when his eye is off me, or his attention distracted from me, and no moment, therefore, when his care falters.
>
> This is momentous knowledge. There is unspeakable comfort . . . in knowing that God is constantly taking knowledge of me in love and watching over me for my good. There is tremendous relief in knowing

4

that his love to me is utterly realistic, based at every point on prior knowledge of the worst about me, so that no discovery now can disillusion him about me, in the way I am so often disillusioned about myself, and quench his determination to bless me.[5]

How encouraging! No one knows us better than God does. He knows what we're going to say even before we say it (Ps. 139:4). He knows the number of days we have left (v. 16). He even knows the number of hairs on our heads (Luke 12:7). Because God knows us so well, the journey toward intimacy with Him may be further along than we think.

Let's keep moving toward Him now by doing a little reflective thinking and writing.

Moving toward Intimacy

What is your current level of intimacy with God? Is it soaring high, or has the wind gone out from beneath your wings? If it's lower than you would like, you don't need to beat yourself down even further. God, as we just read, is ready and waiting to start afresh.

With God's assurance in mind, take some time now to evaluate your level of intimacy with Him.

To begin with, describe your relationship with God. Is it warm and steady? Or has it become interrupted, distracted? Has it grown cold? Does it seem like a deep friendship or a surface acquaintance? Is it active and growing? Or slow and stale? An exciting personal adventure? Or a mechanical routine? In your own words, let your thoughts, and your pen, run free.

_____

_____

_____

_____

_____

5. J. I. Packer, *Knowing God*, 20th anniversary edition (Downers Grove, Ill.: InterVarsity Press, 1993), pp. 41–42.

_____

_____

_____

_____

_____

Do you believe that developing and maintaining intimacy with God is important? Why? What difference does it make (or would it make) in your life—in your view of and confidence in God, the strength of your relationships, the effectiveness of your testimony and ministry?

_____

_____

_____

_____

_____

_____

_____

_____

What would you like to change regarding your relationship with the Lord? How, specifically, would you like this series of lessons to help you draw closer to Him?

_____

_____

_____

_____

Take a few minutes to meditate on the words of the apostle Paul in Philippians 3:2–11. How important was knowing Christ to Paul?

_____

_____

_____

What clues do you find in this passage about Paul's close walk with the Lord?

_____

_____

_____

_____

Does an intimate relationship with God mean a trouble-free life (v. 10)?

_____

_____

_____

Do we ever "arrive" at the perfect intimate relationship with Christ in this life (v. 12)?

_____

_____

_____

Is it possible to know a lot *about* God without really knowing Him (see Matt. 23:1–12; John 14:5–9)?

_____

_____

_____

_____

Think about your closest relationships—spouse, children, parents, siblings, close friends. What has made these relationships so close? Are you more transparent and open with these people than you are with others? Do you spend more time with them? Make a list of activities and attitudes that make these your most intimate relationships.

_____

_____

_____

_____

_____

Now, what can you apply from these relationships that will help you develop greater intimacy with God?

_____

_____

_____

_____

_____

_____

_____

_____

Spend the rest of your reflective time in prayer. Tell God that you long to draw closer to Him. Ask Him to show you things in your life that may be keeping you at a distance. Thank Him for taking the initiative in establishing an intimate relationship with you.

Chapter 2

SIMPLICITY:
REORDERING OUR LIVES

Selected Scriptures

Behold, I stand at the door and knock; if anyone hears My voice and opens the door, I will come in to him, and will dine with him, and he with Me'" (Rev. 3:20). This is the Lord's great invitation to intimacy; to be alone with Him, to enjoy the pleasure of His company over a meal that nourishes both heart and soul.

But can we hear His knocking? Can we hear His voice over the clamor and chaos that all too often fragments our lives?

If His coming to us is drowned out by the din of hurried, cluttered, distracted lives, how then shall we ever become intimate with Him?

What we need is a quiet, focused space in our souls, where there is time and clear-headedness and a vibrant awareness of God's nearness. Deep in your heart, isn't that something you hunger for?

One of the ways to create this environment is through simplicity. What exactly is simplicity? We've called it a discipline and noted that it involves reordering our lives, but how do we do that? To what extent do we need to go?

Let's see if we can answer some of these questions; then we'll try to discern whether the pace and shape of our lives is strangling our relationship with God.

Defining Simplicity

Dallas Willard, in his book *The Spirit of the Disciplines*, defines simplicity as "the arrangement of life around a few consistent purposes, explicitly excluding what is not necessary to human well-being."[1]

Does this mean taking a vow of poverty—casting away our possessions and leading an ascetic life? Not necessarily, though some people would probably sigh with relief to be rid of their material burdens. What we have in mind, however, is something broader, focusing more on those "consistent purposes" Willard mentioned.

---

1. Dallas Willard, *The Spirit of the Disciplines: Understanding How God Changes Lives* (San Francisco, Calif.: Harper and Row, Publishers, 1988), p. 170.

Jesus crystallized them for us in His Sermon on the Mount.

"Seek first His kingdom and His righteousness; and
all these things shall be added to you." (Matt. 6:33)

How do we seek His kingdom? By loving and valuing Him with all our heart, soul, and mind, and by loving our neighbor as ourselves (22:36–40).

Simplicity, then, is bringing these purposes into clear focus and shedding those things that distract us from them. It's living in harmony with our inward desires and outward lives. Or as Anne Morrow Lindbergh wrote, "I would like to achieve a state of inner spiritual grace from which I could function and give as I was meant to in the eye of God."[2]

No small task! What makes this so difficult for us, particularly those of us in America? Certain symptoms may give us a clue to the core problem.

Symptoms of a Simplicity-Deficient Life

If we were to sketch out a pencil portrait of the average American, it might look something like this.

Most of us say yes to too many things. Perhaps because we don't want to disappoint others or because it's easier to let someone else direct our lives, we are busier than we need to be.

Most of us do not plan well enough ahead or think through our schedules to leave time for leisure and rest. By not assuming responsibility for meeting our needs of rest and refreshment, we live passively and become tense and resentful at others' demands. However, we can't blame our mates, our bosses, or our roommates for complicating our lives—because, too frequently, *we* allow it to happen.

Most of us have too many things on our plate to get done in the allotted time. As soon as we finish one thing (sometimes even before we finish), we are on to the next. We rarely take time to know the joy of accomplishment (see Prov. 13:12, 19a).

Most in America have too much debt. And to make matters worse, many of us aren't working our way out of debt but deeper into it. It's not uncommon for a credit card to have as much as $18,000 outstanding. Wow! Rather than money serving our life, we end up

---

2. Anne Morrow Lindbergh, *Gift from the Sea*, 20th anniversary edition (New York, N.Y.: Random House, Vintage Books, 1978), pp. 23–24.

using our energies and talents to serve money's demands. *Most of us fool ourselves into thinking that because we live in a modern world with high-tech equipment, we are simplifying our lives.* Can you program your VCR? (Couldn't resist asking that!) If you lost one of your remotes, would you know how to operate your TV, VCR, or stereo manually? Have you felt compelled to constantly upgrade your computer, adding the latest revved-up software that takes days to learn? Faster, newer, and better doesn't always mean simpler.

Diagnosis of the Core Problem

In 2 Corinthians 11:3, the apostle Paul pinpoints the core condition reflected by all these symptoms:

> I am afraid, lest as the serpent deceived Eve by his craftiness, your minds should be led astray from the simplicity and purity of devotion to Christ.

In other words, Paul says, "My fear is that, as he did with Eve, Satan should seduce you away from a simplicity of devotion to the Savior." Alan Redpath, in his book *Blessings Out of Buffetings*, writes,

> That is an arresting phrase because in these days there is scarcely anything that is simple; everything is so complicated. What am I to believe? What is right? What is wrong? In every area of life the old simplicities have vanished from us until even this word *simple* has changed, and I do not think people like being called *simple* because it has an association that is a little unpleasant! It would mean that you are not quite one-hundred percent! That is not the meaning of the word in the New Testament, for simplicity means single-hearted, crystal clear. . . .
> . . . A man may be a saint without having many of the qualities which the world today rates very highly, but he will never be a saint without the simplicity of soul, a simplicity that is in Christ.[3]

In light of Paul's words and Redpath's illumination of them, take a moment to ask yourself a couple of questions. First, *do you*

---

3. Alan Redpath, *Blessings Out of Buffetings: Studies in II Corinthians* (Westwood, N.J.: Fleming H. Revell Co., 1965), pp. 187–88.

have too much clutter within to leave sufficient room for devotion to Christ? This usually shows up in two ways: too little time for prayer and not enough space to meditate.

Now, you don't need to pray four hours a day; sometimes fifteen minutes will do. Just enough time to push away the temporal pressures that seduce you from eternal reality. And you don't need to learn yoga to meditate; just take time to mull over a thought, look at it from every angle, and if need be, wrestle with it.

And second, *have you begun to get self-impressed or sophisticated about your faith?* Has the serpent seduced you toward pride over the diploma on your wall, your reputation, your intellect, your ability to be in control? God sups with the humble, remember, blessing the poor in spirit with the riches of His grace—because the humble know their need and come to Him with open hands.

Prescriptions for a Simpler Life

If there is any way in the world that Satan can seduce us from a simple, warmhearted, loving devotion to Christ, he'll do it. His craftiness is so subtle that he can steal a seminary student's love for Christ and replace it with a love for the Bible—without the student's even knowing it.

So how can you fight him and keep your focus pure? Not knowing the details of every person's life, we can't really dispense a specific set of actions. However, we can prescribe some questions and guidelines that will help you probe areas needing change.

In Your Own Personal World

Let your spouse, your children, your parents, your friends, your coworkers all fade from your mind right now. It's just your life you are looking at, the individual God made and will call home to Himself one day. Now what thoughts come to mind with the following questions?

1. *Is there something you must do about your time with God?* Some simplifying of your schedule so you can begin meeting with Him, totally alone—no TV, no music, no radio—privately, for just fifteen minutes a day?

2. *Do you need to say no more often?* Do you need to back out of some things you've already said yes to? Is your peace of heart worth risking disappointing others or being less visible? Are you at the mercy of your multiple gifts rather than utilizing them to serve

God through an unfragmented heart? Do you need to plan a way out of debt?

3. *Have you become cluttered in your person?* Is your living space choking out your life? How cluttered is your closet, your desk, the trunk of your car? Are you carrying too much "stuff" with you through life? And how about your mind? Is it cluttered with worry, guilt, fear, busyness? As Henry David Thoreau observed, "Our life is frittered away by detail . . . Simplify, simplify."[4]

In Your World of Relationships

Now step into the realm of your involvements with others, your roles and activities, and consider these questions.

1. *Are the good things keeping you from the best?* Jesus could have taught 120 disciples and traveled farther than Paul; yet He chose to invest His life in only the Twelve and go no farther than two hundred miles from his birthplace (see Mark 1:32–39 for an example of Jesus' singularity of purpose). Thoreau wrote, "Let your affairs be as two or three, and not a hundred or a thousand; instead of a million count half a dozen, and keep your accounts on your thumb-nail."[5]

2. *Are too many things draining your energy, leaving you exhausted—even resentful?* Simplifying may call for selling or giving away some things that you're having to maintain but that you're not using.

3. *Are the activities outside your home stealing time from those within the home?* What will your family remember twenty or thirty years from now—a blur of Little League games, gymnastics practices, choir rehearsals, golf tournaments, overtiredness, and hurryhurryhurry? Or warm relationships, laughter, hugs, and long, quiet walks and talks?

Concluding Counsel

Hopefully, you are not feeling overwhelmed and guilty at this point. That's not our intention at all. Rather, we want to help you see that you are not powerless against the many distractions that threaten to fritter away your life. We want to empower you with the reality that God has given you a great deal of control over what goes on in your life.

4. Henry David Thoreau, as quoted in *Bartlett's Familiar Quotations*, 15th ed., rev. and enl., ed. Emily Morison Beck (Boston, Mass.: Little, Brown and Co., 1980), p. 559.

5. Thoreau, as quoted in *The Columbia Dictionary of Quotations* (New York, N.Y.: Columbia University Press, 1993). From Microsoft Bookshelf ©1987–1994 Microsoft Corporation. All rights reserved.

Living in simplicity does not mean stopping all activities and saying no all the time. But it does involve refusing to excuse any longer the clutter and complication that drains your time and energy. It's reordering your life around nourishing priorities, quieting your heart so you can hear Jesus knocking and let Him in.

Moving toward Intimacy

> Things which matter most must never be at the mercy of things which matter least.[6]
> —Goethe

> The key is not to prioritize what's on your schedule, but to schedule your priorities.[7]
> —Stephen R. Covey

Priorities. We all have them, whether or not we can fully articulate them. We all make decisions—how to spend our time and money, which career to pursue, which relationships to build, the skills we develop—based on what we think is important. The trick is to consistently live life in sync with what *truly* matters.

Putting first things first fosters simplicity. Once we've identified what's important, we can say no to things that aren't. Our lives, then, become a series of deliberate decisions strung together with a strong thread of purpose. If we don't identify and schedule our priorities, however, our decisions are as haphazard as a handful of spilled beads. We spend so much time looking for them and picking them up, we can't arrange them in any sensible order. And how can we take time to gaze into heaven if we're on our hands and knees, looking under the couch for runaway beads?

If you're having a hard time keeping up with all your beads, this is a great opportunity for you to think about what's really important. This could be the first step to simplifying your life and creating a spiritual environment conducive to drawing closer to God.

Start by listing four or five of the most important relationships or activities in your life. Day after day, week after week, these are

---

6. As quoted in Stephen R. Covey, *The Seven Habits of Highly Effective People* (New York, N.Y.: Simon and Schuster, A Fireside Book, 1989), p. 146.

7. Covey, *Seven Habits*, p. 161.

the people and practices most worthy of your time, energy, and thought. They include knowing God better; loving and caring for your spouse, children, and closest friends; staying physically and mentally fit; and so on.

_____

_____

_____

_____

_____

Now, are you taking time to plan these priorities into your schedule each week—*before* your calendar becomes cluttered with urgent (but less important) activities? If not, what changes do you need to make?

_____

_____

_____

Take a close look at your commitments. Are they scattered and unfocused? Are there some that you need to graciously back out of in order to allow time for these precious priorities?

_____

_____

_____

There in the clutter, God is waiting to be found—a priceless Pearl among a mess of scattered beads. Simplify. Seek Him. And He will honor your desire to draw near.

Chapter 3

SILENCE AND SOLITUDE: ESSENTIALS FOR INTIMACY

Selected Scriptures

As the deer pants for the water brooks, So my soul pants for Thee, O God," cried the psalmist (Ps. 42:1). Yearning, longing, thirsting for the Lord's presence, for the fullness of life that comes from intimacy with Him, that's the picture of the psalmist's soul—and our souls too.

Where can we find the pure, refreshing water we need to cool our parched lips? Probably not in more activities, more hubbub, more noise, more thirsty people. Psalm 23 gives us a better idea:

> The Lord is my shepherd,
> I shall not want.
> He makes me lie down in green pastures;
> He leads me beside quiet waters.
> He restores my soul. (vv. 1–3a)

What quietness and attentiveness fill this scene. How tender is the Shepherd, and how cool the drink He offers. Do you see, it is in silence, in solitude, that God comes to restore us to Himself.

Only in silence can we quiet our souls, allowing our hearts to rest like a sleeping child in his mother's arms (see Ps. 131:2). Only in solitude can we center ourselves, settling into God's love and His call on our lives.

Silence and solitude provide sabbaths for us, ways of resting with the purpose of drawing near to God. The first is a sabbath of the mouth; the second, a sabbath of involvements.

Silence

Have you ever stopped to realize that the majority of our communication in relationships is nonverbal? We learn to read the sighs, the slouches, the smiles, and the spring in the steps of those around us. And these silent signals often communicate as much, if not more, than a person's words do.

Silence, as significant as it is, sometimes strikes us as unimportant,

16

uncomfortable, even threatening. So we rush to fill up the spaces with our words. Author Henri Nouwen observes the problem this has caused:

> Over the last few decades we have been inundated by a torrent of words. Wherever we go we are surrounded by words: words softly whispered, loudly proclaimed, or angrily screamed; words spoken, recited, or sung; words on records, in books, on walls, or in the sky; words in many sounds, many colors, or many forms; words to be heard, read, seen, or glanced at; words which flicker off and on, move slowly, dance, jump, or wiggle. Words, words, words! They form the floor, the walls, and the ceiling of our existence. . . .
>
> Recently I was driving through Los Angeles, and suddenly I had the strange sensation of driving through a huge dictionary. Wherever I looked there were words trying to take my eyes from the road. They said, "Use me, take me, buy me, drink me, smell me, touch me, kiss me, sleep with me." In such a world who can maintain respect for words? . . .
>
> The result of this is that the main function of the word, which is communication, is no longer realized. The word no longer communicates, no longer fosters communion, no longer creates community, and therefore no longer gives life.[1]

Sometimes a steady stream of words forms a moat of distance rather than a bridge to community; the verbal clutter we surround our lives with becomes an effective "sound barrier"—from ourselves, others, and God. Starting today, let's learn to value the richness of silence and the opportunities it creates.

What Does Silence Create?

What does silence create for us? It

- makes room for listening

- gives us the freedom to observe

1. Henri J. M. Nouwen, *The Way of the Heart* (New York, N.Y.: Random House, Ballantine Books, 1981), pp. 31–32.

- allows time to think

- provides space to feel

- lets us broaden our awareness

- opens us to the entry of peace

- invites us to know our limitedness . . . and God's vastness

Silence, writes Cornelius Plantinga, Jr., offers those who wisely choose it "a quiet place in which they are at home with themselves, in touch with God, and hospitable to the voices of others."[2]

Have your words ever brought you as close to another as a meaningfully shared silence?

Biblical Perspectives on Silence

The Bible is replete with silences. For example, there is the silence that is appropriate before God's majesty:

> "The Lord is in His holy temple.
> Let all the earth be silent before Him."
> (Hab. 2:20; see also Zeph. 1:7; Zech. 2:13)

What better reflects our reverence and awe than our speechlessness? The hymnwriter knew this:

> Let all mortal flesh keep silence,
> And with fear and trembling stand;
> Ponder nothing worldly minded,
> For with blessing in His hand
> Christ our God to earth descendeth,
> Our full homage to demand. . . .
>
> At His feet the six-winged seraph;
> Cherubim with watchful eye,
> Veil their faces to His Presence,
> As with ceaseless voice they cry,
> "Alleluia, Alleluia,
> Alleluia, Lord most high!"[3]

2. Cornelius Plantinga, Jr., "Background Noise," in *Christianity Today*, July 17, 1995.

3. "Let All Mortal Flesh Keep Silence," liturgy of St. James, trans. Gerard Moultrie, in *Hymns for the Family of God* (Nashville, Tenn.: Paragon Associates, 1976), no. 166.

Only when our mouths are closed and our minds quiet can we begin to grasp God's immense greatness and hear the angels' Alleluias.

In Exodus 14, we find another benefit of keeping still. Here the newly freed Israelites have just left Egypt, only to be trapped between the Red Sea and a vengeful Pharaoh's approaching army. Panic ensues—and so does grumbling. "'Is it because there were no graves in Egypt that you have taken us away to die in the wilderness?'" they accuse Moses. "'It would have been better for us to serve the Egyptians than to die in the wilderness,'" the Israelites conclude (vv. 11a, 12b).

Moses has more faith in God, though, and tells them, "'Do not fear! Stand by and see the salvation of the Lord which He will accomplish for you today. . . . The Lord will fight for you while you keep silent'" (vv. 13a, 14).

When we stop fussing and start trusting, we will be able to see that God is more deeply at work in our lives than we ever imagined.

A third scriptural purpose of silence is connected with Solomon's counsel in Proverbs 4:23,

> Watch over your heart with all diligence,
> For from it flow the springs of life.

One of the most effective ways of watching over our hearts lies in discretion. *Webster's* defines *discreet* as being "capable of preserving prudent silence."[4] We sometimes worry so much about *what* to say that we don't stop to consider *if* we should speak at all. As Solomon says further on,

> The one who guards his mouth preserves his life;
> The one who opens wide his lips comes to ruin.
> (13:3; see also 10:19; 15:28; 17:28; 21:23)

Samson was one who neither watched over his heart nor preserved a prudent silence. Entangled in a lust-love relationship with the treacherous Delilah, Samson made a fatal error: "He told her all that was in his heart" (Judg. 16:17). She, in turn, told his enemies, who captured him, bound him, and gouged out his eyes (vv. 18–21).

A lot of things in our hearts we have no business telling a soul. Special words from the Lord; our deepest dreams, thoughts, hopes. They are precious and deserve to be kept safe by the guardian of silence.

---

4. *Merriam-Webster's Collegiate Dictionary*, 10th ed., see "discreet."

If we refuse to provide pockets of silence in our lives, we will always flounder in a fog, wondering who God is and what He's doing. We will remain shallow. But if we deliberately fashion protracted periods of silence, we will grow deeper in an increasing awareness of the real presence of God.

Shhh. Stop and let this soak in. We've provided some lines for you to write down whatever comes to mind.

_____

_____

_____

_____

_____

_____

_____

_____

Solitude

Solitude, like its partner silence, rewards us with a depth seldom found through other means. However, solitude may be one of the most difficult disciplines to practice, because so many of us are afraid to be alone. Anne Morrow Lindbergh has crystallized our dilemma.

> How one hates to think of oneself as alone. How one avoids it. It seems to imply rejection or unpopularity. An early wallflower panic still clings to the word. One will be left, one fears, sitting in a straight-backed chair *alone*, while the popular girls are already chosen and spinning around the dance floor with their hot-palmed partners. We seem so frightened today of being alone that we never let it happen. Even if family, friends, and movies should fail, there is still the radio or television to fill up the void. Women, who used to complain of loneliness, need never be alone any more. We can do our housework with soap-opera heroes at our side. Even daydreaming was more creative than this; it demanded

something of oneself and it fed the inner life. Now, instead of planting our solitude with our own dream blossoms, we choke the space with continuous music, chatter, and companionship to which we do not even listen. It is simply there to fill the vacuum. When the noise stops there is no inner music to take its place. We must re-learn to be alone.[5]

What does solitude, this sabbath of involvements, have to offer us?

What Does Solitude Create?

Solitude allows us to rest; it gets us away from the constant push and pull of others' demands, interruptions, schedules, and expectations. In solitude we

- discover our own thoughts

- filter out the nonessentials

- find our own pace

- rest and regroup

- recall the meaning of our unique call

- hone and clarify what we value

- gain perspective

- reinforce our focus

- reacquaint ourselves with our dreams

- become more attentive to God

Solitude uncovers layer after layer of our life, driving us deeper and deeper to the core. God does not leave us to dig alone; He's at the top layer, and He's waiting at the core. What we discover may be troubling—who knew we had so many fears, so much sin, so much sadness, so much criticism of ourselves and others? But solitude urges that we keep reaching, because God's hand of grace keeps reaching out to us.

Once we clasp His hand and realize His forgiveness, His peace

5. Anne Morrow Lindbergh, *Gift from the Sea*, 20th anniversary edition (New York, N.Y.: Random House, Vintage Books, 1975), pp. 41–42.

washes over our hearts like a light spring rain. Ultimately, it is this spiritual serenity that we cultivate in solitude. We seek a calm, restful center from which we can gather strength to participate more fully in life.

Biblical Perspectives on Solitude

Even Jesus needed solitude. Mark's gospel describes a day in His life when He taught in the Capernaum synagogue, confronted and cast out a demon, healed Peter's mother-in-law, then cast out more demons and healed more people (Mark 1:21–34). Mark says, "The whole city had gathered at the door" (v. 33)!

In the midst of the immediacy and the pressure of everyone's needs, notice that Jesus still took the time to be alone.

> Very early in the morning, while it was still dark,
> Jesus got up, left the house and went off to a solitary
> place, where he prayed. (v. 35 NIV)

He knew He could not minister to others from a scattered, fragmented, unfocused heart. Only alone with God could His purposes and strength be refreshed.[6]

It's hard to hear God in a crowd. As Elijah found, God often comes not in earthquake and fire but in the "sound of a gentle blowing" (1 Kings 19:12). Or as commentator C. F. Keil put it, "It was in a soft, gentle rustling that He revealed Himself to him."[7]

A soft rustling is much easier to hear in solitude.

Concluding Thoughts

Silence and solitude, our twin means of God-directed rest, offer us essential moments of sanity amidst the craziness of life. Concerning silence, *since it is the gateway to depth, it's worth every effort to make it happen.* Can you carve out an hour or two, perhaps an afternoon or even a whole day, to refrain from speaking, escape from noise, and quiet your soul? Like a rest in a piece of music, the silence helps define the significance of the sound.

---

6. Note what the apostle Paul said about his own preparation for ministry: "I did not immediately consult with flesh and blood, . . . but I went away to Arabia, and . . . three years later I went up to Jerusalem to become acquainted with Cephas" (Gal. 1:16–18).

7. C. F. Keil, *The Books of the Kings*, trans. James Martin, in Biblical Commentary on the Old Testament series, by C. F. Keil and F. Delitzsch (Grand Rapids, Mich.: William B. Eerdmans Publishing Co., n.d.), p. 258.

And concerning solitude, *since it is the gateway to discovery, it is too important to ignore.* One of the most meaningful ways of preserving what you learn in solitude is to journal. You don't necessarily need a computer to do this; in fact, a book might even be better in case you have photos, letters, or mementos you want to keep with your thoughts. A journal differs from a diary or daily planner in that you don't write in it every day—it will get shallow if you do. Rather, your journal records your journey with God.

Silence and solitude invite us to drink deeply of God's presence, helping to slake the thirst of a panting soul.

Moving toward Intimacy

> We need to find God, and he cannot be found in noise and restlessness. God is the friend of silence. See how nature—trees, flowers, grass—grows in silence; see the stars, the moon and the sun, how they move in silence. . . . We need silence to be able to touch souls.
>
> —Mother Teresa[8]

Silence, as Mother Teresa observed, benefits more than the one being silent. It is a means to the end of ministering to others. How can we keep the flame of ministry burning without the fuel that silence provides? And how can we carry Living Water to others, if we don't stop first at the well to refresh our own souls?

Have you stopped at the well lately? You may be surprised at how much more impact you'll have in the lives of others if you'll alternate times of Christian activity with interludes of silence.

Determine to carve out some quiet solitude for yourself this week. Take a look at your schedule. Pick a day. Set aside an hour or two. Go ahead, write it down; make it firm.

8. Mother Teresa, as quoted in *The Columbia Dictionary of Quotations* (New York, N.Y.: Columbia University Press, 1993). From Microsoft Bookshelf © 1987–1994 Microsoft Corporation. All rights reserved.

Now, where will you go for this time of silent solitude? Do you need to get away from the house? Get to the office early, before anyone arrives? You might even want to spend this time outdoors.

_____

_____

What will you take with you? Your Bible, most likely. How about a hymnal? Journal and pen, perhaps?

_____

_____

After your retreat, keep a record of how God uses you in the lives of those closest to you. When the dust of activity makes you a little dry, go back to the well and drink.

Chapter 4

SURRENDER: INTIMACY REQUIRES LETTING GO

Selected Scriptures

Getting close sometimes means letting go.

When your wife picks you up at the airport after a long business trip, you need to drop your luggage before you can hug her. And when your two-year-old son runs to greet you, it's a lot easier to pick him up if you set down your briefcase.

God made our hands—and our hearts—able to hold only so much. If we hang on to too many things, or the wrong things, we can distance ourselves from what's really important.

Paul showed us what's most important when he wrote,

> I count everything as loss compared to the possession of the priceless privilege (the overwhelming preciousness, the surpassing worth, and supreme advantage) of knowing Christ Jesus my Lord and of progressively becoming more deeply and intimately acquainted with Him [of perceiving and recognizing and understanding Him more fully and clearly]. (Phil. 3:8a AMPLIFIED)

Closeness with God, you see, also requires our willingness to turn loose of interests that keep us at arm's length from Him. That's called surrender. And it's our fourth discipline in this study for fostering intimacy with the Almighty.

Surrender Means Letting Go

The writer of Hebrews knew how hard it was to embrace Christ with arms full of excess baggage. That's why he said,

> Let us also lay aside every encumbrance, and the sin which so easily entangles us, and let us run with endurance the race that is set before us. (Heb. 12:1)

Let's carefully consider his instruction to determine what we need to surrender.

25

Lightening the Load

First, notice the word order of that verse. We're to lighten our load *before* we run the race. Running with endurance depends on our casting off unnecessary weight. We're to throw off "every encumbrance," that is, anything that hinders us in the spiritual race.

What are some of the things that weigh us down on our way to God? For example, too much television. Too many activities and involvements. Too much time and effort spent on unfruitful relationships with difficult people. Encumbrances can be any number of things, including comparing ourselves to others—and their encumbrances!

Just as athletes watch tapes of themselves in action, so we need to take a close look at our form to rid ourselves of the bulk that's slowing us down.

Shedding "The Sin"

The "sin which so easily entangles us" possibly refers to one specific sin rather than generalities. Given the context of chapters 11 and 12, which highlights faith, it suggests the sin of unbelief, or not trusting God.

Chapter 11, after all, is full of the faithful. The vivid testimonies of Noah, Abraham, Sarah, Moses, Rahab, and others surround us. They speak to us from the past to encourage us in our present walk of faith. By following their example, and truly trusting God, we can avoid the sin of unbelief.

Surrender Means Focusing on Christ

Shedding our encumbrances and sin is only half the battle. If we let go of one thing, we have to hold on to something, or Someone, else. The writer of Hebrews tells us where that focus needs to be:

> fixing our eyes on Jesus, the author and perfecter of faith, who for the joy set before Him endured the cross, despising the shame, and has sat down at the right hand of the throne of God. (Heb. 12:2)

Christ Our Example

Focusing on Christ—that's the key, because He is the ultimate model of surrender. Jesus let go of heaven to bring us to God; we must let go of earth to stay close to God. Paul pointed this out to the Philippians in his plea for them to live in unity and humility.

Do nothing from selfishness or empty conceit, but with humility of mind let each of you regard one another as more important than himself; do not merely look out for your own personal interests, but also for the interests of others. Have this attitude in yourselves which was also in Christ Jesus. (Phil. 2:3–4)

The phrase "humility of mind" in verse 3 is one word in the Greek. Author David Jeremiah provides some interesting insight on the term.

The word translated "[humility] of mind" was transformed by the impact of the Christian Gospel. Before Christ came, that word was viewed as a negative character trait, for it was associated with weakness and cowardliness. When Christ came, He taught His disciples how to submit to one another out of love instead of fear.[1]

Do you want a definitive picture of humility? Paul says, "Take a look at how Christ lived . . . and died."

Although He existed in the form of God, [He] did not regard equality with God a thing to be grasped, but emptied Himself, taking the form of a bond-servant, and being made in the likeness of men. And being found in appearance as a man, He humbled Himself by becoming obedient to the point of death, even death on a cross. Therefore also God highly exalted Him, and bestowed on Him the name which is above every name, that at the name of Jesus every knee should bow, of those who are in heaven, and on earth, and under the earth, and that every tongue should confess that Jesus Christ is Lord, to the glory of God the Father. (vv. 6–11)

Mind-boggling, isn't it? The Lord of the Universe, King of all Creation. The object of the angels' worship. He emptied Himself, which essentially means He surrendered the independent use of His divine attributes. He didn't stop being God, but He voluntarily limited the use of His prerogatives as deity. He even experienced death. And He did it for us. That's humility!

1. David Jeremiah, *Turning Toward Joy* (Wheaton, Ill.: Scripture Press Publications, Victor Books, 1992), pp. 66–67.

Only truly humble people can surrender, because they see themselves in light of something or Someone greater. The Father's will was Jesus' passion; the redemption of humanity His goal. That kept Him humble, focused, and close to the Father.

Don't Despair . . . Compare

Focusing on Christ not only connects us with His strength and reminds us of His surrender, it provides perspective for those times when we wonder why we signed on for the Christian life. In those hard places, we need to follow the advice of the writer of Hebrews and "consider" our Savior.

> For consider Him who has endured such hostility by
> sinners against Himself, so that you may not grow
> weary and lose heart. (Heb. 12:3)

The Greek word for *consider* conveys the idea of comparison.[2] When mistreatment, misunderstanding, and other kinds of adversity come our way, this passage exhorts us to think about the Lord of heaven, who voluntarily suffered at the hands of sinful men. Since our good and God's glory came out of His hardship, we can be encouraged that whatever we face will ultimately be for our good as well (see Rom. 8:28).

When we focus on Christ—trusting in His strength, following His example, considering His suffering—we can begin to understand what surrender is all about.

Four Areas of Surrender

Tossing aside unnecessary spiritual baggage and focusing on Christ, however, doesn't mean that surrender is always easy. If we were to be honest, most of us probably struggle with letting go of four things: our possessions, our position, our plans, and our people.

Our Possessions

You don't have to own a lot to be attached to it. You can own one old, broken down bicycle, but if it occupies more of your time, attention, and devotion than Christ does, it needs to be surrendered. However, the more we possess, the more opportunities we

---

2. F. F. Bruce, *The Epistle to the Hebrews* (Grand Rapids, Mich.: William B. Eerdmans Publishing Co., 1964), p. 355.

have to fill our hands and hearts with something besides Christ.

Letting go of possessions, though, doesn't necessarily mean we have to part with them altogether. We just need to keep them in proper perspective. That's what A. W. Tozer asked for when he prayed,

> Father, I want to know Thee, but my cowardly heart fears to give up its toys. I cannot part with them without inward bleeding, and I do not try to hide from Thee the terror of the parting. I come trembling, but I do come. Please root from my heart all those things which I have cherished so long and which have become a very part of my living self, so that Thou mayest enter and dwell there without a rival. Then shalt Thou make the place of Thy feet glorious. Then shall my heart have no need of the sun to shine in it, for Thyself wilt be the light of it, and there shall be no night there. In Jesus' name. Amen.[3]

Our Position

Clutching our positions too tightly can also hinder intimacy with God. If we're not careful, we can look to our job for our security. Titles, accomplishments, and recognition bring strokes. If we start living for those strokes instead of longing for the Savior, we're moving away from intimacy with Him. Our sense of worth and importance should rest in Christ, because He loves us, He died for us, and we are His treasured possession, bonded to Him eternally through faith. Our destiny is secure because of His faithfulness. That's something we can hold on to.

Our Plans

Are your hopes and expectations based on life turning out as you planned? James warned us against trusting too much in our design for the future.

> Come now, you who say, "Today or tomorrow, we shall go to such and such a city, and spend a year there and engage in business and make a profit." Yet you do not know what your life will be like tomorrow. You are just a vapor that appears for a little

3. A. W. Tozer, *The Pursuit of God* (Camp Hill, Pa.: Christian Publications, 1982), pp. 30–31.

while and then vanishes away. Instead, you ought to say, "If the Lord wills, we shall live and also do this or that." (James 4:13–15)

James doesn't mean we shouldn't plan, set goals, or cultivate vision. But we must do all these activities realizing that God is the one who ultimately directs our steps (see Prov. 16:9). Asking Him to direct *our* plans, however, isn't the way to intimacy. Discovering His plan and seeing Him carry it to completion through us is what brings us closer to Him.

Our People

God has placed people around us to help us along life's path and, hopefully, teach us something about Himself. Though we hold them dear, we should hold them loosely. Our children, spouse, parents, and dearest friends, after all, belong to Him. And none of them were ever meant to fill the space that only He can fill.

Surrender. You'll discover surprises you would never have known otherwise. And you'll know Christ better than you ever thought you could.

 ## *Moving toward Intimacy*

"Cease striving and know that I am God," says the Lord (Ps. 46:10). How many times have we heard that verse? Yet do we really know what it means? What did the psalmist have in mind?

"Cease striving" is one word in the Hebrew, *raphah*. The root means "sink" or "relax." The same word appears in Psalm 37:8:

> *Cease* from anger, and forsake wrath;
> Do not fret, it leads only to evildoing.
> (emphasis added)

Raphah suggests inactivity, relying on God's strength instead of ours. "Stop doing what you're doing, and look to God," in other words. We might even say, "Surrender."

Have you noticed that we tend to surrender last the things we think we can handle ourselves? Most of us don't have a problem, for example, leaving our salvation to God. We know we can't save ourselves; that's His department. But how often do we surrender the temptation to hate someone who has wronged us? How quick are we to turn over the purchase of a new home to the Lord? Or a job change? Or a father-to-son or mother-to-daughter chat? We even think we can keep juggling all those balls in our circus-like schedule without dropping one.

It's time we took a little Hebrew lesson: *Raphah*. Stop. Give it to Him. Trust His strength, His perspective, His will. Not just for the big things, but for everything.

Take an inventory of the things you need to surrender to God. List the decisions, relationships, personal struggles, etc., that you know He can handle better than you can.

_____

_____

_____

_____

_____

Now, why do you think God is better equipped to handle them than you are?

_____

_____

_____

Think about what you have coming up this next week, the next day, the next hour. See anything else that you need to release?

_____

_____

_____

Now spend some time in prayerful surrender. In fact, make it a habit. Remember, in the spiritual life, getting close means letting go.

BOOKS FOR
PROBING FURTHER

This short series is just one of many rest stops that provide refreshment and reflection along the road to intimacy with God. Many authors have provided cool patches of shade for reflecting on God's goodness, His love, His blessings, and His sufficiency. From the following works, you should be able to find help in learning more about our heavenly Father, as well as reshaping your environment to include Him more.

Blackaby, Henry T., and Claude V. King. *Experiencing God: How to Live the Full Adventure of Knowing and Doing the Will of God.* Nashville, Tenn.: Broadman and Holman Publishers, 1994.

Crabb, Larry, Jr. *Finding God.* Grand Rapids, Mich.: Zondervan Publishing House, 1993.

Dobson, Edward G. *Simplicity: Finding Order, Freedom, and Fulfillment for Your Life.* Grand Rapids, Mich.: Zondervan Publishing House, 1995.

Edwards, Jonathan. *Jonathan Edwards on Knowing Christ.* Carlisle, Pa.: Banner of Truth Trust, 1993.

———. *Religious Affections.* Abridged ed. Portland, Oreg.: Multnomah Press, 1984.

Eyre, Stephen D. *Drawing Close to God: The Essentials of a Dynamic Quiet Time.* Downers Grove, Ill.: InterVarsity Press, 1995.

Foster, Richard J. *Celebration of Discipline: The Path to Spiritual Growth.* Revised ed. San Francisco, Calif.: Harper and Row, Publishers, 1988.

———. *Freedom of Simplicity.* San Francisco, Calif.: Harper and Row, Publishers, 1981.

Gire, Ken. *Windows to the Soul: Experiencing God in New Ways.* Grand Rapids, Mich.: Zondervan Publishing House, 1996.

Hughes, R. Kent. *Disciplines of a Godly Man.* Wheaton, Ill.: Good News Publishers, Crossway Books, 1991.

Lindbergh, Anne Morrow. *Gift from the Sea.* Twentieth anniversary edition. New York, N.Y.: Random House, Vintage Books, 1975.

Nouwen, Henri J. M. *The Way of the Heart: Desert Spirituality and Contemporary Ministry.* New York, N.Y.: Seabury Press, 1981.

Packer, J. I. *Knowing God.* Twentieth anniversary ed. Downers Grove, Ill.: InterVarsity Press, 1993.

Peterson, Eugene H. *The Contemplative Pastor: Returning to the Art of Spiritual Direction.* Grand Rapids, Mich.: William B. Eerdmans Publishing Co., 1989.

Pink, Arthur W. *The Attributes of God.* Grand Rapids, Mich.: Baker Book House, 1975.

Piper, John. *Desiring God: Meditations of a Christian Hedonist.* Portland, Oreg.: Multnomah Press, 1986.

Sproul, R. C. *The Soul's Quest for God.* Wheaton, Ill.: Tyndale House Publishers, 1992.

Tada, Joni Eareckson. *A Quiet Place in a Crazy World: Drawing Near to God Through Prayer and Praise.* Sisters, Oreg.: Questar Publishers, Multnomah Books, 1993.

Tozer, A. W. *The Pursuit of God.* Camp Hill, Pa.: Christian Publications, 1982.

Whitney, Donald S. *Spiritual Disciplines for the Christian Life.* Colorado Springs, Colo.: NavPress, 1991.

Willard, Dallas. *The Spirit of the Disciplines: Understanding How God Changes Lives.* San Francisco, Calif.: Harper and Row, Publishers, 1988.

Some of these books may be out of print and available only through a library. For those currently available, please contact your local Christian bookstore. Books by Charles R. Swindoll may be obtained through Insight for Living. IFL also offers some books by other authors—please note the ordering information that follows and contact the office that serves you.

NOTES

NOTES

NOTES

NOTES

NOTES

NOTES

ORDERING INFORMATION

INTIMACY WITH THE ALMIGHTY

If you would like to order additional study guides, purchase the cassette series that accompanies this guide, or request our product catalogs, please contact the office that serves you.

United States and International locations:

Insight for Living
Post Office Box 69000
Anaheim, CA 92817-0900

1-800-772-8888, 24 hours a day, seven days a week
(714) 575-5000, 8:00 A.M. to 4:30 P.M., Pacific time, Monday to Friday

Canada:

Insight for Living Ministries
Post Office Box 2510
Vancouver, BC, Canada V6B 3W7

1-800-663-7639, 24 hours a day, seven days a week

Australia:

Insight for Living, Inc.
General Post Office Box 2823 EE
Melbourne, VIC 3001, Australia

Toll-free 1800-772-888 or (03) 9877-4277, 8:30 A.M. to 5:00 P.M., Monday to Friday

World Wide Web:
www.insight.org

Study Guide Subscription Program

Study guide subscriptions are available. Please call or write the office nearest you to find out how you can receive our study guides on a regular basis.